YOUR KNOWLEDGE HAS VALUE

- We will publish your bachelor's and master's thesis, essays and papers

- Your own eBook and book - sold worldwide in all relevant shops

- Earn money with each sale

Upload your text at www.GRIN.com and publish for free

Jens Saathoff

The British Parliament - How the Powers of Parliament and those of the Government are balanced

GRIN Verlag

Bibliografische Information der Deutschen Nationalbibliothek:

Die Deutsche Bibliothek verzeichnet diese Publikation in der Deutschen National-
bibliografie; detaillierte bibliografische Daten sind im Internet über http://dnb.d-
nb.de/ abrufbar.

Imprint:

Copyright © 1992 GRIN Verlag GmbH
Druck und Bindung: Books on Demand GmbH, Norderstedt Germany
ISBN: 978-3-656-27873-3

This book at GRIN:

http://www.grin.com/en/e-book/199938/the-british-parliament-how-the-powers-
of-parliament-and-those-of-the

The British Parliament

by Jens Saathoff

Contents

1. Introduction

This paper is about the British Parliament, which constitutes such a wide range of topics that some selected aspects have to be concentrated on. For that reason the political function of the British Crown will be neglected. The main aim of this essay will be to find out how the powers of Parliament and those of the Government are balanced. It is assumed that the powers of making und passing laws und the control of the executive are indicators of this problem.

First of all, the role that Parliament plays in the British Constitution will be defined. In this context it will be important to note that the British Constitution as such does not exist in writing, which raises the question as to whether this fact causes any negative consequences for the democratic process. Moreover, the structure and composition as well as the functions of the two Houses of Parliament will be dealt with. And some characteristic features of the parliamentary system in Britain will be pointed out in order to draw a comparison between the British and the German Parliament. Of course, this comparison will have to focus on the most significant aspects. In the final part the preceding considerations will be summarized and a personal judgement on the two different systems in Britain and Germany will be made.

2. Which role does Parliament play in the British Constitution?

It has to be emphasized that Britain as opposed to most other countries does not have a written constitution. Basically the British Constitution consists of three elements, namely "Statute Law", "Common Law" and "customs"[1]. Statutes are enacted by Parliament and are put down in writing. Acts of Parliament are, for example, the "Bill of Rights of 1689" or the "People Acts of 1948 and 1949".[2] These Acts of Parliament do not necessarily refer to constitutional aspects, but some of them concern the Constitution in so far as they define the powers and limits of particular institutions, for instance, of the House of Lords. Yet they do not determine the relations between all the institutions of the state and thus do not meet the requirements of a constitution on their own. So the other elements are of constitutional significance, too. "Common Law" is not

---

[1] Sydney D. Bailey: British parliamentary democracy, 1978, p. 2.
[2] Anthony H. Birch: The British system of government, 1991, p. 21.

written down in any statutes, but consists of judicial decisions which establish precedents for later judgements and in this way can establish constitutional rights. Of course, customs are not written down either. Nevertheless they play an important part in the British Constitution. It is, for example, constitutional customs that the Sovereign does not take part in the Cabinet's assemblies and does not reject bills the two Houses of Parliament have agreed to and passed.[3]

Apart from the elements "Statute Law", "Common Law" and "customs" there are some features of the British Constitution I would like to mention briefly. Firstly, the United Kingdom is not a federal state as the Federal Republic of Germany is, but a unitary one. As a result of this fact the local government in the United Kingdom receives its powers and is dependent on the enactment of the Westminster Parliament. Secondly, the Prime Minister and his Cabinet are responsible to Parliament. And finally, the political parties have an important function in the parliamentary system of Britain.[4]

As to the role Parliament plays in the British Constitution it can be said that its legislative powers are not limited by any influence of the courts of law. That means that enactments by Parliament cannot be declared unconstitutional, which makes an important difference to the German system. In Germany a law passed by the "Bundestag" could be judged unconstitutional by the "Bundesverfassungsgericht", for example, if it does not comply with the personal rights every citizen is guaranteed. Consequently, this law will have to be changed or at least altered. The obviously strong position of Parliament concerning legislation leads to the question as to what the relationship between Parliament and the Administration looks like. To what extent does Parliament control the executive part of the Government? Has it got a strong position here as well?

As already mentioned above the Ministers are responsible to Parliament. Not only does the Ministers' resonsibility refer to their actions, but also to the "actions of their departments"[5]. If Parliament does not approve of a Minister's policy and loses confidence in him, the Minister will be forced to resign. So the executive is also controlled by Parliament. Since the House of Commons, the most powerful one of the two chambers, is elected by the people, the strong position of Parliament ensures that the political system of Britain works democratically. Although there is no denying the fact that the House of Commons is an important democratic device and plays a powerful role in the British Constitution, there are some factors to be found in the system of government which are not under the direct control of Parliament. First of all the influence of the British Crown

---

[3] Sydney D. Bailey: British parliamentary democracy, 1978, p. 4.
[4] Ibid., pp. 5,6.

has to be mentioned. Ministers are appointed and the meetings of the House of Commons can only be convened by the Monarch. However, it has to be admitted that these rights of the Monarch's are executed on the advice of the Prime Minister. A more important limit to the powers of Parliament is the fact that the Government can make decisions in foreign policy without parliamentary assent. Treaties with foreign countries need not be ratified by Parliament; nor is it up to the decision of Parliament whether war should be declared or not. The declaration of war is a decision the Prime Minister has to take.[6] Contrary to the British system in Germany the ratification of the "Bundestag" is necessary in either case.

But of course these governmental powers do not make the British political system undemocratic. As the Government is supported by the majority of an elected parliament, its policy is in a way justified by a democratic election. The composition of the House of Commons is determined by a general election. For that reason the decision which party obtains the right to form a government is made on a democratic basis. Of course, it could be doubted whether an unwritten constitution is appropriate for guaranteeing democracy in a state. But the political system in Britain seems to show that a nation's attitude towards and experience with a parliamentary system is of more importance than the written text of a state's constitution.[7]

Taking the aspects mentioned so far into account there are two different views of the role of the British Parliament. On the one hand the legislature is very potent, since it is not affected by any judicial decisions. Furthermore, Parliament can call the Ministers to account for their own and their departments' actions whereby it controls the executive. On the other hand Parliament as such does not have the possibility of deciding about the Government's policies. Moreover, there is still the political influence of the British Crown. And it should not be forgotten that the second chamber, though it does not possess as many rights as the House of Commons, is not an elected one. In this paragraph some characteristics of Britain's Constitution and their influence on the role of Parliament have been dealt with. The following section will go into the details of the chamber's composition and functions. At the same time a comparison between the British and the German parliamentary systems will be drawn.

---

[5] Anthony H. Birch: The British system of government, 1991, p. 22.
[6] Anthony H. Birch: The British system of government, pp. 23-25.
[7] Sydney D. Bailey: British parliamentary democracy, 1978, p. 7.

3. The British Parliament

The British Parliament consists of an elected chamber, the House of Commons, and the House of Lords, whose members are mostly hereditary peers and life peers.

3.1 The House of Lords

One function of the House of Lords is a judicial one, since the Upper Chamber is the "supreme judicial tribunal of the nation"[8]. This function comprises the hearing of appeals, which is exercised by a special committee of the House of Lords. Another task of the House of Lords, which is perhaps more important, is to study, revise and amend bills already passed by the Lower Chamber. The Lords can also delay the passing of a bill for one year at the most. Of course the opinions about this possibility of delaying vary. The opponents of this right of the Lords' claim that it could slow down the democratic process of legislation at a time, when certain events would require a quick political reaction. On the other hand the Lords can use their power to ensure that there is enough time for the electorate to inform themselves about the intended bill and to express their opinions on it. But in fact the Commons have some possibilities of forcing the Upper Chamber to pass the bill. Furthermore bills concerning financial matters are entirely controlled by the Commons. The revision of bills by the Lords can also have a positive effect in so far as peers are not dependent on any party line. Nor are they responsible to the electorate. That means that they can really express their own view on a subject. Therefore I think the existing situation is very useful.

Apart from dealing with subjects raised by the Lower Chamber the House of Lords can also introduce bills itself. Though this right does not refer to bills which are too controversial. Unlike the House of Commons, which does its work under pressure, the Upper Chamber has sufficient time to discuss important topics at length, which is in my opinion a necessary process in political life and thus another significant task. The House of Lords has more than 1100 members. This number includes hereditary peers, peers appointed for life and some office-holders as bishops and Law Lords.[9] In Germany the "Bundesrat" represents the governments of the "Bundesländer". As a result of this fact its composition is determined by democratic elections. In Britain it is impossible to con-

---

[8] Sydney D. Bailey: British parliamentary democracy, p. 36.
[9] Ibid., p. 29.

stitute the second chamber in the same way as in Germany, since the United Kingdom is a unitary state. The existence of a second chamber which is not elected has often been criticized in Britain, because it does not seem to fit in a democratic state. If the House of Lords as it exists at the moment was definitely thought inappropriate for a democratic state, there would be two possibilities of changing the system. Either the House of Lords could be replaced by an elected chamber or it could be completely abolished. If the House of Lords became a chamber elected democratically, it would certainly claim to receive the same rights as the Lower Chamber, because it would have the same legitimacy. But there is no use in having two Houses of equal powers. On the other hand an abolition of the House of Lords would mean that there is no longer an institution which prevents Parliament from pushing bills through hurriedly.

In my opinion it is very important for the electorate that there are still discussions on political subjects which do not only show the attitudes of parties, but express personal judgements. Germany is an example of a political system where party influence is to be found everywhere, even in fields where it should not play any role. Nevertheless I think that the Upper Chamber should not have the possibility of doing any harm to the democratic process. But there is no point in abolishing the House of Lords and the advantages of such a chamber as well; it would mean throwing the baby out with the bathwater. In conclusion, it is useful to preserve the merits of a second chamber on condition that democracy is not curtailed.

3.2 The House of Commons

The House of Commons consists of 651 Members of Parliament, whose main functions can be divided into three different fields. They have to pass or reject bills introduced to Parliament, to deal with the nation's finances, an important part of which is the yearly budget statement, to debate motions tabled in the House and last but not least to criticize and control the Government. The Speaker of the House is the person who has to see to it that discussions are held according to the rules. Generally he may be called the "spokesman"[10] of the House of Commons, because he also functions as a representative. On account of his role the Speaker is expected to hold an impartial point of view. Accordingly he does not take part in a political debate, nor does he express his preference for a certain party. And finally it deserves mentioning that the role of the Speaker and

---

[10] Sydney D. Bailey: British parliamentary democracy, p. 63.

also some other rules of Parliament as, for example, the way of voting date back to the beginnings of the parliamentary system in Britain.

With regard to legislation it has to be asked whether it is a power really exercised by Parliament or whether it is the Government that dominates the legislative process. Interestingly enough, most bills are introduced by the executive. Of course, the House of Commons, whose majority supports the Government, will seldom reject a bill the Administration is in favour of. Moreover, it should be pointed out that legislation is not only determined by elected politicians, but also influenced by very strong interest or pressure groups. It is difficult to say how important the pressure groups' influence really is. But as a matter of fact the Government and interest groups often have negotiations before a bill is presented to Parliament.[11] This evokes the impression that Parliament has only the right to confirm what the Government has negotiated beforehand. Furthermore, the existence of party whips makes sure that the results of votes are normally to the liking of the party leaders. That means that Members of Parliament are not totally free in their voting (however, there are not always three-line whips). Of course, Members of Parliament have the possibility of expressing their dissent with the party line. But if they do so, they will have to take the consequences. To put it in another way, votes in Parliament are often very predictable and not the result of individual opinions. Thus there is no peed for a Government to fear that its own proposals will be rejected.[12]

According to Sontheimer in Germany most bills are also introduced by the Government.[13] In contrast to the Westminster Parliament the "Bundestag" has a stronger influence on the making of laws in so far as it sends representatives to the committees which are constituted to draft bills. For that reason the committees try to include also the Opposition's opinion in their planning. And although there is a party line in Germany, too, it is not as strong as in Britain.

It has already been pointed out here that there is a strong governmental position. This is partly due to the fact that the British Parliament has hardly any influence on the policies and decision-making of the Government; on top of that the electoral system in Britain is regarded as a reason for this. According to the existing electoral system (first past the post) the parliamentary seats are not distributed in proportion to the votes received by the parties. A party does not need the absolute, but only the simple majority of seats to form the Government. On the other hand this system has the advantage that a general election always brings a clear-cut result, which means that there is no need for a coali-

---

[11] Philip Norton: The changing nature of the House of Commons, 1987, pp. 71, 72.
[12] Ibid., p. 78.

tion.[14] Thus it is different from the German system, where it is very seldom that one party can form the Government on its own. Notwithstanding this possible advantage the electoral system helps to create an executive which might be considered too powerful. Owing to all these considerations it is not amazing that there have been efforts to establish institutions which possess the right and ability to influence governmental work. As a result of this in 1979 the "Select Committees"[15] came into being. These Committees have had the function to scrutinize and to examine government departments, and they have proved effective in doing so. However, the rights of these Committees are restricted to examination and do not include the possibility of forcing the Government to act in a certain way so that there is not a far-reaching influence on the executive.

As for the control of the Government it has to be said that the German "Bundestag" has not got many possibilities either. The most useful means of control in Germany seems to be the "Untersuchungsausschuß", which shows similarities to the Select Committees in Britain, since it has also the function to scrutinize governmental affairs. The composition of the "Untersuchungsausschuß" reflects the composition of the "Bundestag". Consequently most members of this committee support the Government and are not interested in criticizing their own party. The same, of course, applies to the British committees, too.

4. Conclusion

Britain does not have a written constitution (although some parts of it are set down in writing) as opposed to most other countries. Owing to the considerations above it can be said that this fact does not cause any serious problems for the democratic process in Britain. In my opinion, however, the advantage of a written constitution like the German one could be that it is a basis on which parliamentary decisions can be judged. But British courts do not even have the right to declare Acts of Parliament unconstitutional. So the British Parliament seems to obtain far-reaching powers. On the other hand legislation is more or less under the controlling influence of the Government, which is partly justified by the Government's majority in the House of Commons and partly incompatible with the function of Parliament.

---

[13] K. Sontheimer: Grundzüge des politischen Systems der BRD, 1973, p. 141.
[14] Philip Norton: The changing nature of the House of Commons, 1987, p. 77.
[15] Ibid., pp. 80-83.

As to the possibility of exerting influence on the Government it has to be said that Parliament holds a relatively weak position. Except for the right to call the Ministers to responsibility there are not many means to bring pressure to bear on the Government. Among others it is an important thing that treaties with foreign countries need not be ratified by the House of Commons. Of course the electoral system contributes much to the strength of the Administration, but I do not dare to say whether this is a disadvantage or a merit. In comparison with the House of Commons the "Bundestag" seems to have some more possibilities of taking part in the process of making laws. Otherwise it also holds a rather weak position except for the fact that its ratification of treaties is needed. With regard to the House of Lords we can say that this chamber is a useful institution, at least in a unitary state. The political system in Germany shows that it is sometimes necessary to see a point of view that is totally independent of a party line.

Finally, I would like to point out that I do not prefer one system or the other. Both systems have their advantages and drawbacks; and above all their historical development must also be taken into account. But Great Britain has one advantage Germany will never be able to compensate for. The British democracy has existed for a comparatively long time and has turned out to be viable, whereas the Federal Republic of Germany is young and still has to offer evidence of her ability to survive.

Bibliography

Bailey, Sydney D.: British parliamentary democracy. 3rd ed. Greenwood Press: Westport, Connecticut 1978.

Birch, Anthony H.: The British system of government. 8th revised ed. 1991, Harper Collins Academic, London.

Norton, Philip: The changing nature of the House of Commons: external challenges - internal reinforcements, in: Döring, Herbert u. Dieter Grosser (Hrsg.): Großbritannien. Ein Regierungssystem in der Belastungsprobe. Opladen: Leske 1987, pp. 69-85.

Sontheimer, K.: Grundzüge des politischen Systems in der Bundesrepublik Deutschland. 3rd revised ed. Munich: Piper 1973.